# Ancient ROME

## THE BRITISH MUSEUM
### A BOOK OF POSTCARDS

*Pomegranate*

SAN FRANCISCO

Pomegranate Communications, Inc.
Box 808022, Petaluma, California 94975
800-227-1428
www.pomegranate.com

Pomegranate Europe Ltd.
Unit 1, Heathcote Business Centre
Hurlbutt Road, Warwick, Warwickshire CV34 6TD, U.K.

ISBN 0-7649-2469-9
Pomegranate Catalog No. AA200

© 2003 Trustees of The British Museum, London

Pomegranate publishes books of
postcards on a wide range of subjects.
Please contact the publisher for more information.

Cover designed by Lisa Alban
Printed in China
12 11 10 09 08 07 06 05 04 03    10 9 8 7 6 5 4 3 2 1

To facilitate detachment of the postcards from this book, fold each card along its perforation line before tearing.

FAR FROM BEING MONOLITHIC, ancient Roman civilization comprised a variety of subcultures. A tremendous diversity of peoples had settled in Italy by the early Iron Age (ninth–eighth centuries B.C.). These groups—such as the Daunians and Etruscans, whose artisanry is represented in this book of postcards—were eventually united under Roman rule, which took the form of a republic after the last Roman king was expelled in 509 B.C. As the city-state expanded its sphere of influence through treaty, trade, and war, it tended not to suppress the beliefs and practices of those it came to govern (with the notable exception of the early Christians) but to assimilate them. The Romans' openness to outside influences is perhaps best exemplified by their embracing of Greek culture. Roman generals had begun to collect classical art from conquered Greek cities and sanctuaries; this fashion soon spread to the wealthy, who commissioned marble copies of Greek bronzes for their homes and gardens— such as the *Discobolus* featured here. The Romans' taste for things Greek extended beyond art to include Greek literature, religion, and philosophy.

During the reign of Augustus (27 B.C.–A.D. 14)—depicted on the Blacas Cameo wearing the aegis of the goddess Minerva—Rome adopted an imperial system of rule. By the late first century A.D., the Roman empire, as it could now be called, included fifty million inhabitants, its vast territories reaching their greatest extent under the emperor Trajan (whose portrait also appears here). In the distant provinces, Roman presence inevitably transformed the native cultures, but, in turn, the indigenous people came to influence the Romans. Many of the objects in The

British Museum's unparalleled collection of Romano-British antiquities—several of which are included in this selection—illustrate this mutual influence with an interesting blend of Celtic and classic elements.

In the third century A.D., the very existence of the empire was threatened by a combination of economic crisis, internecine struggles for power, and foreign invasions. Diocletian (reigned A.D. 284–305) managed to restore stability by dividing the empire into eastern and western halves, which were in turn subdivided into more easily administered units. Even greater changes were instituted by Constantine I, "the Great" (reigned A.D. 306–37). A convert to Christianity, Constantine gained control of both halves of the empire, moved the Roman capital to Byzantium (which he renamed Constantinople), and made Christianity the official religion. Despite his temporary reunification of the empire, the division between east and west deepened with time. Finally, under waves of barbarian incursions, the western Roman empire collapsed in the fifth century. (Constantinople would remain the capital of the eastern empire for almost another thousand years.) The fall of Rome ushered in the so-called Dark Ages of Europe. Nevertheless, the Romans' cultural legacy—their extensive system of roads, their broad dissemination of common values, and Constantine's promotion of Christianity, for example—would continue to be felt for centuries to come.

# Ancient **ROME**

Bucchero ware chalice
Etruscan, 600–575 B.C.
Probably made in Tarquinia (ancient Etruria), Lazio, Italy
H: 14 cm; D: 16.5 cm
The British Museum GR 1867.5-8.846

BOX 808022　PETALUMA　CA 94975

Pomegranate

*Ancient* **ROME**

The *Discobolus*
Roman copy of a Greek fifth-century-B.C. original
From Hadrian's Villa in Tivoli, Lazio, Italy
H: 1.7 m
The British Museum GR 1805.7-3.43

BOX 808022   PETALUMA   CA 94975

Pomegranate

# _Ancient_ **ROME**

Decorated pottery _askos_
Daunian, c. 350–325 B.C.
From Canosa, Puglia, Italy
H: 33 cm
The British Museum GR 1850.8-23.1

BOX 808022   PETALUMA   CA 94975

Pomegranate

# Ancient ROME

Black-glaze pourer *(askos)* in form of an elephant
Roman, fourth–third century B.C.
From Vulci (now Lazio, Italy)
L: 15.5 cm
Durand Collection
The British Museum GR 1849.6-20.4

BOX 808022    PETALUMA    CA 94975

Pomegranate

# *Ancient* **ROME**

The Great Torc from Snettisham
Iron Age, c. 75 B.C.
Found at Ken Hill, Snettisham, Norfolk, England
D: 20 cm; Wt: 1080 g
Gift of the National Art Collections Fund
The British Museum P&EE 1951 4·2 2

BOX 808022    PETALUMA    CA 94975

Pomegranate

# Ancient ROME

Limestone head of a woman resembling Cleopatra VII
Roman, c. 50–30 B.C.
Acquired in Italy
H: 28 cm
Castellani Collection
The British Museum GR 1879.7-12.15

BOX 808022   PETALUMA   CA 94975

Pomegranate

# *Ancient* ROME

Marble funerary relief of Lucius Antistius Sarculo
and Antistia Plutia
Roman, c. 10 B.C.–A.D. 30
From Rome
H: 63.5 cm; W: 98 cm
The British Museum GR 1858.8-19.2

CA 94975

PETALUMA

BOX 808022

*Pomegranate*

# *Ancient* **ROME**

Bronzed gladiator's helmet
Roman, first century A.D.
Allegedly from Pompeii
H: 46 cm
Purchased with the assistance of Miss H. R. Levy
The British Museum GR 1946.5-14.1

# *Ancient* ROME

Bronze head of the emperor Claudius
Roman Britain, first century A.D.
Found at the River Alde at Rendham, near Saxmundham, Suffolk
H: 30 cm
The British Museum P&EE 1965 12-11

BOX 808022   PETALUMA   CA 94975

Pomegranate

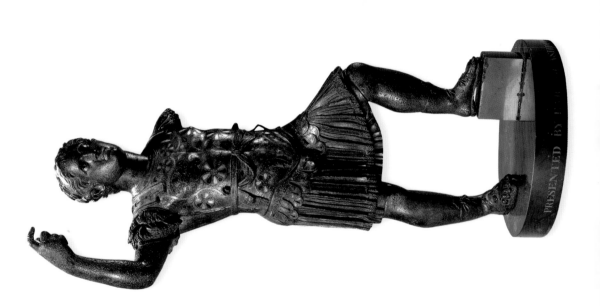

# *Ancient* ROME

Bronze statuette of Nero
Roman Britain, first century A.D.
Probably from Baylham Mill, near Ipswich
H: 56 cm
Gift of the Earl of Ashburnham
The British Museum P&EE 1813.2-13.1

BOX 808022    PETALUMA    CA 94975

*Pomegranate*

# *Ancient* ROME

Bronze model of a two-horse chariot *(biga)*
Roman, first–second century A.D.
Allegedly found in the River Tiber, Rome
H: 20.5 cm; L: 25.5 cm
The British Museum GR 1894.10-30.1

BOX 808022   PETALUMA   CA 94975

*Pomegranate*

# *Ancient* ROME

Terracotta figurine of two gladiators
Roman, first—second century A.D.
H: 12.8 cm
The British Museum GR 1907.5-18.4

BOX 808022  PETALUMA  CA 94975

Pomegranate

# Ancient ROME

Marble statue of a youth on horseback
Roman, A.D. 1–50
Made in Italy
H: about 206 cm
Formerly in the del Bufalo and Farnese collections, Rome
The British Museum GR 1864.19-21.2

BOX 808022    PETALUMA    CA 94975

Pomegranate

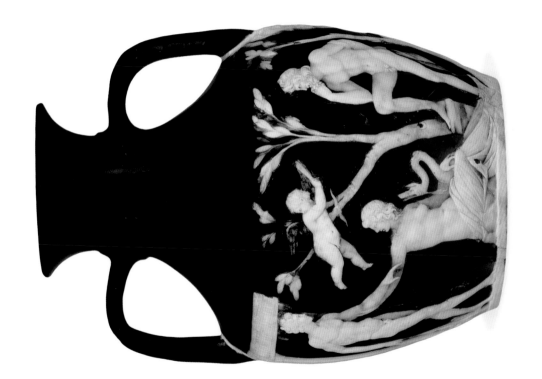

# *Ancient* ROME

The Portland Vase
Perhaps from Rome, c. A.D. 5–25
H: 24 cm; D: 17.7 cm
Purchased with the aid of a bequest from James Rose Vallentin
The British Museum GR 1945.9-27.1

BOX 808022   PETALUMA   CA 94975

Pomegranate

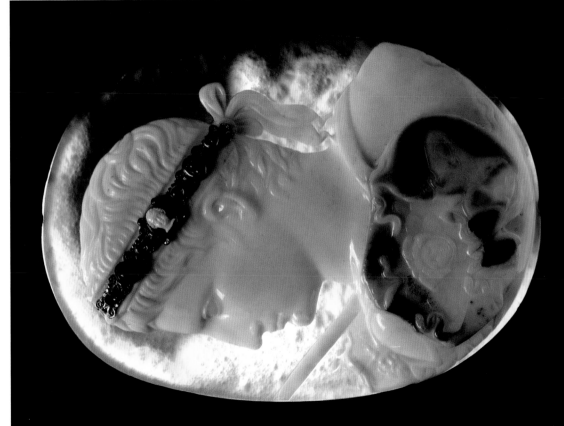

# *Ancient* ROME

Cameo portrait of Augustus (The Blacas Cameo)
Carved from a three-layered sardonyx
Roman, c. A.D. 14–20
H: 12.8 cm; W: 9.3 cm
Strozzi and Blacas Collections
The British Museum GR 1867.5-7.484

BOX 808022  PETALUMA  CA 94975

*Pomegranate*

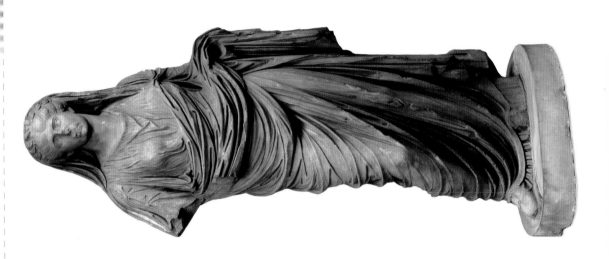

# Ancient **ROME**

Marble statue of a Roman priestess
Roman, c. A.D. 20–50
From Atrapaldo, southern Italy
H: about 205.75 cm
Castellani Collection
The British Museum GR 1873.8-20.741

BOX 808022  PETALUMA  CA 94975

Pomegranate

# Ancient ROME

Marble portrait of Julius Caesar
Roman, c. A.D. 50
From the Sanctuary of Athena in Priene, Turkey
H: 39.5 cm
The British Museum GR 1870.3-20.201

BOX 808022    PETALUMA    CA 94975

Pomegranate

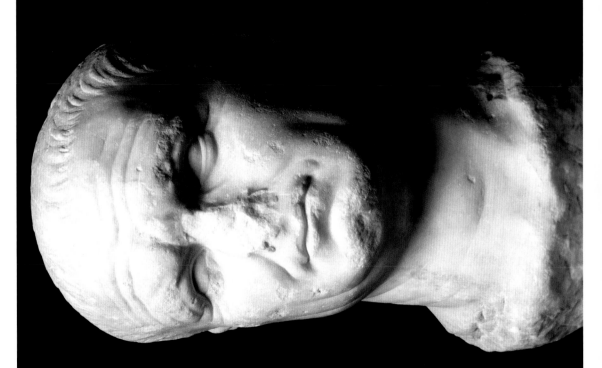

# *Ancient* ROME

Head from a marble statue of Vespasian
Roman, A.D. 70–80
From Carthage, northern Africa (modern Tunisia)
H: 45.5 cm
Excavated by Sir Thomas Reade
The British Museum GR 1850.3-4.35

BOX 808022   PETALUMA   CA 94975

*Pomegranate*

# *Ancient* ROME

Brass *sestertius* of Titus, showing the Colosseum
Roman, A.D. 80–81
Minted at Rome
D: 31 mm; Wt: 23.36 g
The British Museum CM 1844.4-25.712

BOX 808022    PETALUMA    CA 94975

Pomegranate

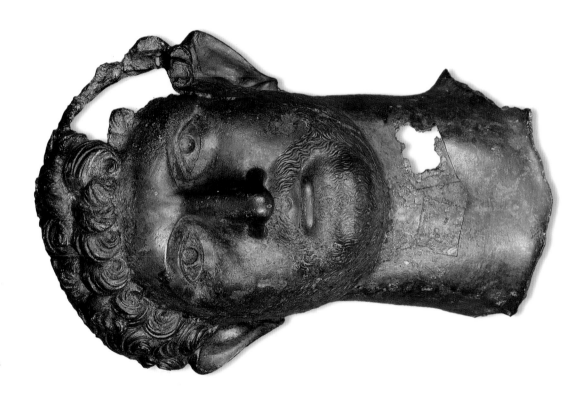

# *Ancient* ROME

Bronze head from a statue of the emperor Hadrian
Roman Britain, second century A.D.
Found in the River Thames near London Bridge (1834)
H: 43 cm
The British Museum P&EE 1848 11-3 1

BOX 808022   PETALUMA   CA 94975

*Pomegranate*

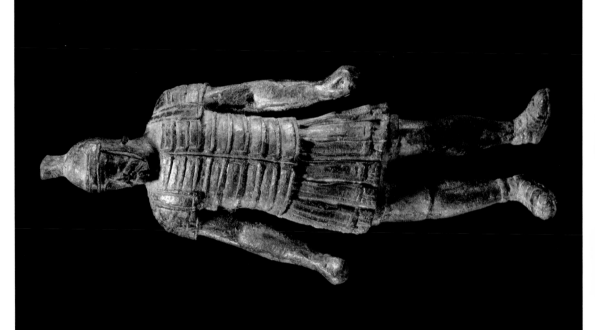

# Ancient **ROME**

Bronze statuette of a legionary
Roman, second century A.D.
H: 11.5 cm
Castellani Collection
The British Museum GR 1867.5-10.4

BOX 808022  PETALUMA  CA 94975

Pomegranate

# *Ancient* ROME

Marble group of Mithras slaying the bull
Roman, second century A.D.
From Rome
H: 133 cm
The British Museum GR 1825.6-13.1

BOX 808022 PETALUMA CA 94975

*Pomegranate*

# *Ancient* ROME

Marble statue of a naked Aphrodite crouching at her bath
Roman, second century A.D.
H: 1.12 m
On loan from Her Majesty the Queen
The British Museum GR 1963.10-29.1

BOX 808022    PETALUMA    CA 94975

Pomegranate

# *Ancient* ROME

Marble statue of Venus
Roman, c. A.D. 100–150
Found at Campo Iemini, near Torvaianica, Lazio, Italy
H: 223.5 cm
Gift of King William IV
The British Museum GR 1834.3-1.1

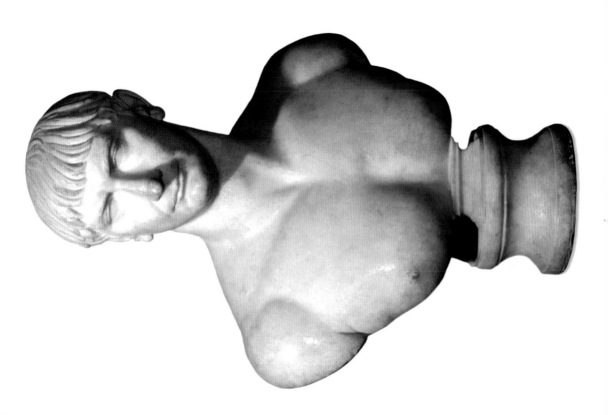

## *Ancient* **ROME**

Marble bust of Trajan
Roman, c. A.D. 108–117
Made in Italy
H: 68.5 cm
Bequeathed by Charles Townley
The British Museum GR 1874.7-12.11

BOX 808022  PETALUMA  CA 94975

*Pomegranate*

# *Ancient* ROME

Marble statue of the emperor Septimius Severus
Roman, c. A.D. 193–200
Found at Alexandria, Egypt
H: 198 cm
Gift of King George III
The British Museum GR 1802.7-10.2

BOX 808022    PETALUMA    CA 94975

Pomegranate

# *Ancient* **ROME**

The Bank of England mosaic
Roman Britain, third century A.D.
Found under the Bank of England, London
H: 1.5 m; W: 1.5 m
Gift of the Governor and Directors of the Bank of England
The British Museum P&EE 1806.11-15.1

BOX 808022  PETALUMA  CA 94975

*Pomegranate*

# *Ancient* **ROME**

Coin-set pendant
Late Antique, fourth century A.D.
Probably from Constantinople (modern Istanbul)
H: 90 mm; W: 92.4 mm; Wt: 63.14 g
Purchased with the assistance of the National Art Collections Fund
The British Museum M&ME 1984.5-1.1

BOX 808022   PETALUMA   CA 94975

Pomegranate

# *Ancient* ROME

The Great Dish from the Mildenhall treasure
Roman Britain, fourth century A.D.
Found in Mildenhall, Suffolk
D: 60.5 cm; Wt: 8256 g
The British Museum P&EE 1946 10-7 1

BOX 808022    PETALUMA    CA 94975

*Pomegranate*

# Ancient **ROME**

Gold "lion hunt" plaque
Late Antique, fourth century A.D.
From Asia Minor (modern Turkey)
H: 5.01 cm; W: 5.01 cm; Wt: 66.87 g
Bequeathed by Sir A. W. Franks
The British Museum M&ME AF.332

BOX 808022   PETALUMA   CA 94975

Pomegranate